"Walk tall in your
own truth. It is the
light-glow of the Inner
Presence~Infinity"

Kieran Flynn, RSM

Time for What Matters

Living a Legacy in the 21st Century

Cynthia V. Mitchell

Published by LP Publishing

4737 N. Ocean Drive

Ft. Lauderdale, FL 33308

ISBN: 978-0-9827232-7-2

Printed in the United States

Acknowledgments

Gratitude is the blessing of the Soul upon those you appreciate; and in that spirit, I want to thank those without whom this book would have remained only thoughts in the pages of my mind.

In honor of:
The Spirit of God which bids me to reflect upon my inner life:
"Enter unhestitatingly Beloved, for in this abode there is naught but my love   and longing for Thee"(The Abode Chapel).

My Beloved husband, editor and sage, you encouraged me to write; and this book is the result of your devotion to my process:
You are my eternal love.

My soul sister, Catherine, if ever there were complementary energies in the world then we are them. Your willingness to type and review these thoughts, and to be there always:
"I carry your heart with me,I carry it in my heart" e.e. Cummings

Dear Mother and Father, your love for one another and our family, inspires me to this day. You taught me to treasure each moment and always remember:
Love never ends.(1Corinthians 13)

My family and friends, my business mentors and advocates, teachers, clients and patients, my business partners, you who have shaped my life by your daring to live your legacy now:
"We do not change as we grew older; we simply become more clearly ourselves."
(Lynn Hall)

My spiritual mentors. especially from Our Lady of Peace Spiritual Life Center, Rhode Island, the Sufi community at The Abode, New York, and my Unity experience, southwest and southeast Florida.

My marketing and branding coaches, Kellie and Cliff, my book cover designer, Sabrina, and my webmaster Sye, all whose encouragement and support are gifts I will remember always .

May all of you and all of our readers be blessed by our intention of gratitude and may these words inspire you to make "time for what matters" the legacy you live now!

Time for What Matters

Living a Legacy in the 21st Century

Contents

"Cynthia lives by the principles
of Truth with heartfelt compassion
and deep faith. She has taught me
for twenty years that my mind either
works for me or against me. You will
be changed by reading her book
and following her plan for success, joy
and love – just as I have!"

Foreword

I coined the term "can con" when I was about to play a key tennis match and stepped onto the court and saw my opponent was 40 years my junior! I felt my stomach do flip-flops as I was grabbed by the thought: "How CAN I ever WIN?" I centered myself and took control of those doubting thoughts. I breathed deeply, and imagined that I was 40 years younger, and that I would play with the resilience of someone that age. I call this the "CAN CON" dance and I know it works. Not only did I win the match, I received one of the best compliments of my career as a tennis player. After the match, my young opponent said, "Someday, with enough training, I hope to play like you did!"

Baby Boomers are no strangers to challenges like these in every facet of their lives. And at this time of planning for retirement or entering retirement, while the world economy is so unstable and so challenging, boomers are called upon to do the "Can Con" dance. If boomers want a better quality of health and wellbeing, along with the financial means to live that life, they will have to strengthen their belief that they CAN make the necessary changes that will be required of them so that they too can come out on the winning side.

Cynthia V. Mitchell, a boomer herself, offers the way to make those changes happen NOW. Ever since I met her several years ago in Naples, Florida, I have watched her career growth with great interest. I recognized her skills as an entrepreneur, public speaker, and organizational leader. Her work on the challenges facing boomers in retirement so impressed me that I invited her to speak to my classes on entrepreneurship at Hodges University, where I am now professor emeritus. She is both challenging and engaging, informed and stimulating. And oh, that hearty laugh! I would recognize her in a crowded room at the Oscars! She has certainly gained the respect of her peers in all her endeavors, as evidenced by the many positions she has held and the awards she has received.

Her founding ownership of several businesses over the years, including two pioneering holistic counseling centers, a successful wellness business, a very popular bed and breakfast, and an expanding wedding-planning business, demonstrates her versatility as a consummate entrepreneur. She has been especially involved in encouraging female-owned businesses, an influence recognized through her presidency of her local women's networking association and her regional and national business-woman-of-the-year awards.

Cynthia reminds me of the adage: "A mind becomes innovative only after an idea is transformed into action." What you will experience with her as you travel through this book is an inspiring story and a plan of action that will make your senior years safe, secure, and solvent.

Yours prosperously,
Dr. Gene Landrum
Founder, Chuck E. Cheese
Professor Emeritus, Hodges University

"It is never too late
to be what you
might have been."

George Eliot
(Mary Ann Evans)

Introduction

Have you ever wondered how you can live the good life and have time for what matters? Have you ever found yourself reflecting upon what really matters to you and how you can prioritize it? What would you do differently if time and money weren't major issues? Would you:

- Spend more quality time with your family?
- Exercise?
- Vacation more?
- Work less or not at all?
- Pursue your passions?
- Volunteer more?

Early "baby boomers," like myself (born 1949), have been asking the question "Where do we go from here?" At every phase of our lives, from early school years to the current day, as we enter into our sixties. Those of us born between 1946 and 1954, the first half of the boomer generation, are perhaps more conscious of the significance of that question now because we believe we are more in charge of our future than previous generations. We have more choices and more possibilities ahead of us if we can leverage the *time* to enjoy them.

It seems clear from recent surveys of early boomers reported in About.com *Senior Living*, that we share three overall concerns:

- Maintaining healthier lives that will extend our longevity and reduce our dependency on steadily increasing health-care costs;
- Having that extra income per month that will make us financially comfortable and reduce the fear of running out of money during retirement;
- Making informed decisions about how and where we want to live out our later years, so we reduce the possibilities of experiencing our worst nightmare—living alone in a nursing home as a ward of the state.

I would add a fourth concern, which I will call "conscious living." This reflects my own perspective on life, and perhaps reflects your values also. I express this through the concepts of "conscious retirement" and "living a legacy," increasing the richness of one's inner life.

Most recent surveys omit probing boomers' inner lives, the spiritual dimension, which I believe many of you hold to be of prime importance. Although you may indeed feel the reality of health challenges, income strategies, and residential choices, living a legacy makes us aware of who we are becoming along the journey of life. Conscious retirement, while mindful of what we have accomplished, is not necessarily defined by our accomplishments.

If you, too, have been exploring these concerns, please join me as I share answers that may inspire you to achieve peace of mind and live your vision of the good life now. Time, indeed, may mean money, but money is only the means to experiencing the dreams we value most. Living a prosperous life has little directly to do with money and everything to do with having balanced, healthy, and fulfilling experiences through which we can transform lives for the better.

According to the Social Security Administration, at the age of 65...

- 1% of Americans will be very rich—like Bill Gates, Donald Trump, and the Walton family.
- 7 to 8% will be financially secure—money in the bank, savings, retirement income, and a comfortable life.

But the real shocker is that...

- At age 65, more than 90% of Americans will suffer from the stress of <u>not</u> being in a position to retire.

We see this enfolding all around us...

- Loved ones dying before their time because of unnecessary "Dis-ease."
- Friends working two and three jobs just to get by.
- Elderly folks going back to work, when they should be enjoying living their legacy.

You may not be able to apply for a permanent life insurance policy at this time in your life or afford long-term care insurance, but, as the old saying goes, "If you fail to plan you definitely plan to fail." Give yourself permission to change and appreciate the power of cumulative action.

The purpose of this book is to help you to create your vision and take action *to ensure that you live your dream now* by setting a new or revised direction for a journey over which you have control. After reflecting on my situation and searching for answers, I faced the task of figuring out a way to unlock "The Prosperity Code." I believe I have found such a key, and want to share it with you.

First, I will share how I came to appreciate the need for planning ahead. Second, we'll examine the range of challenges we face in our 60s and beyond, and how we might frame solutions to these challenges through experiencing the process of creating prosperity. The final two chapters outline the principles of prosperity that you can discover through exploring conscious retirement and living a legacy. Understanding how to use these principles can be your guide to true prosperity. Follow my story, learn from it what you can...and prosper.

"Live as if you were
to die tomorrow.
Learn as if you were
to live forever."

Mahatma Gandhi

Chapter 1

Planning for Prosperity

What is prosperity to you? Is it a feeling? A state of mind? The quality of your life; your health; your relationships? Is it static or a dynamic state toward which we are always moving?

For me, prosperity is a way of being in the flow of life.

Prosperity = total wellbeing.

Our pre-"senior" years between 48 and 65 are years that financial professionals call years of "accumulation." Our senior years, 65-plus, are typically years of "disbursement" of our savings. I see those renewal years, between 48 and 65, as opportunities to accumulate prosperity as income, as time freedom, wisdom, and as enriching every facet of our lives.

According to a report by McKinsey and Co., a financial services company, more than *65% of all baby boomers are totally unprepared for retirement.* They have no Plan B, no savings, no clear path ahead of them, and no balance in their lives. They have assumed that things would take care of themselves, that income would continue to flow, and that life would remain relatively unchanged. This appears to be true even for many of us who had successful careers before retirement.

My husband, Bob, and I challenged these findings many years ago, when we decided that there had to be a better way. We began to explore "Conscious Retirement"—ways of making money with a compounding effect that could ultimately provide us lasting income long after we had invested our time. We also took all of our years in the holistic and wellness industries and began traveling the country to educate people on simple ways to ensure long-term health and vitality.

Although we had worked hard our entire lives, we were unwilling to end up in the 90% category with those over age 65 unable to retire. One thing is certain, however, we boomers who have discovered the power of successful careers, now seek to create deeper meaning in our lives. This development is the key to author Ken Dychtwald's assertion in his book, *Age Power*, that our new definition of success is dependent upon us creating a new life of significance. Others refer to this as creating "lives of meaning."

I found the inspiration for this new life, my "Plan B," of wellness, reliable income, and prioritizing my time, in a most unexpected place. My epiphany came through the voices of women in an oncology unit in a Rhode Island hospital. I was invited to speak on spirituality and cancer at the hospital's annual conference. For 25 years, I had trained and practiced as a counselor, a spiritual trainer, and as a meditative retreat organizer. I also owned and operated two holistic counseling centers focused on healing families, couples, and individuals. Yet, this invitation was both a privilege and a challenge because it helped me to continue to integrate both the inner and outer dimensions of my life.

As a result of my presentation, I was asked to facilitate a spiritual insight program in the hospital's oncology unit. This program would become part of an alternative healing strategy for cancer patients. It was this experience that changed my life and encouraged me to examine my own future.

I asked the women in the unit a critical question: "What will you do differently now that you have met the challenge of this disease?" The collective response was: "I would make time for what really matters." These women, I now realize, were my teachers, inspiring me to think long and hard about what mattered most to me. And, much to my surprise, while blessed by my awards and accomplishments, what mattered most to me was none of these.

Throughout my upbringing, I had been taught that a good education would ensure financial stability and that at the heart of success were my accomplishments as a female business owner. These beliefs were especially important during my formative entrepreneurial years in the early 1980's. I had always been driven to work hard and achieve more; after all, wasn't "more is better" the mantra of the times? Yet, I was still evaluating my life primarily from the outside in and not acknowledging my inner spiritual core.

There is a Rule of Discernment in spiritual direction that encourages a person to look for the difference, not between the perceived good and "the better." I had met my soul-sister, Catherine, while organizing a retreat in 1984 and it was with her that I established my counseling centers.

We earned good incomes, led comfortable lives, and subsequently bought a 100-year-old Victorian home in Narragansett, R.I., across from the ocean. This home would become our sanctuary, a place to retreat from the demands of our work. We discovered, soon after our purchase, that the roof needed to be repaired all the way back to the rafters. We needed an immediate Plan B to pay for this extraordinary expense. Out of this challenge was born Ocean Road Bed & Breakfast, which not only paid for the roof but also for a full interior restoration of our home.

Never ones to rest on our laurels, we needed to do better. We had two chronic challenges. First, we faced the "revolving door phenomenon" in our counseling centers. After some of the therapists we had trained worked with us for a while, they would announce that they were setting up their own private practices. Most often, because of the bond created between therapist and client, this meant the immediate loss of a substantial income because clients would follow their therapist to his or her "private" practices. Consequently, we had to spend time, energy, and money training new therapists and rebuilding our client base in order to maintain, let alone to grow, the centers financially.

Second, we had no renewable income, no Plan B. Our incomes were transactional. We were paid for each client visit and, once clients left our center permanently, we no longer received any income from them. Many people are challenged by this "exchanging time for dollars" model. They live from paycheck to paycheck, give no thought to a long-term back-up plan until a crisis strikes, and they are unable to provide a successful "bed and breakfast" solution.

One day, after working in the hospital oncology unit, I asked myself, "If I was not a therapist owning two counseling centers, what would I be doing with my time?" I realized from the bed and breakfast experience that, beyond my SEP/IRA, I had no long-term, residual income that would be available to "pay me" from the counseling services that I provided. I wanted a residual income, similar to those brokers who provided our insurance coverage and were being paid ongoing compensation for signing us onto a policy one time only. When I asked our resource manager about my concern, he guided me to a pension planner. This event crystallized my shift away from a life of defining success based on accomplishments to a journey mindful of what really mattered to me.

New Rites of Passage - The Renewal Age

Researchers have divided our human journey into five main stages or phases: birth, puberty, maturity, old age, and death. Societies long have recognized these stages with sets of rituals or rites of passage: baptisms, confirmations, and initiations into adulthood, weddings, funerals, and the like.

Baby boomers, in part because of their sheer numbers (more than 75 million born between 1946 and 1964) have experienced and transformed many of these rites in their journeys through life. Born during a long post-war period of economic prosperity, many boomers were raised in the new suburbia with single-family homes, new schools, and new consumerism. We were accustomed to being catered to as marketers and media encouraged and molded our tastes in music (rock 'n' roll), clothes, cars, and entertainment (T.V. and movies).

We married at rapid rates and, by the late 1970s and early 1980s, we were divorcing and remarrying at record rates, transforming the social and demographic landscapes of America. As the first boomers reached 65 in 2011, we have redefined "old age." We are living longer and in larger numbers than any previous generation and view the end of life as a stage far away in time. We believe that we are more active, think younger, and look forward to a "renewal age" rather than inevitable old age. In other words, we embrace longevity, good health, and the prevention of disease.

Ah, but here's the rub. Are we really prepared physically, mentally, financially, and spiritually for this extended journey? Many members of our parents' generation survived only with the direct help of their children. Indeed, we were expected to be there for our parents. But in these challenging times, who will be there for us? What quality of life will we have? Seeking answers to these questions encouraged me to go inward and to explore how we need to plan for the challenges ahead.

For me, the key to planning was to have a vision of what I wanted my life to look like for the foreseeable future and to create a strategy that would take me there. My *vision* was to live by the ocean and to maintain a balanced outer life of time freedom, reduced workload, active social involvement, and an inner life of peace, joy, and tranquility. My *strategy* was to create streams of income that would allow me to leverage my time and achieve my vision to live well and prosper. This meant rethinking the meaning of the word PROSPER.

In working with my colleagues, this acronym seemed to capture the essence of the Prosperity Code:

Preparing for
Retirement by
Optimizing
Spiritual principles
Prevention of disease
Environmental awareness
Residual income

I invite you to rekindle the spirit of adventure that characterized the boomer generation and will continue to do so as we make choices that ensure our legacy of health and prosperity.

"The first time
someone shows
you who they are,
believe them."

Maya Angelou

Chapter 2

Optimizing Wellbeing

There is a wonderful song title that captures how many of us early boomers feel when we reach the possibility of "retirement": "Look What They've Done to My Song, Ma." The tone of retirement is changing as we reach our 60s. What do we want the next phase of our lives to look like? And what are the major challenges to that dream? This chapter will explore our principal challenges and how we might resolve them.

Not all early boomers would answer these challenges in a similar manner. According to several researchers, we seem to fall into one or more of five categories:

- **Empowered Trailblazers**: Those who view retirement as a new phase of "involvement" and creativity rather than one of relaxation and disengagement
- **Wealth Builders**: Those whose focus is on careful management of their financial assets in order to create a growing retirement paycheck that will keep them comfortable for the rest of their lives.
- **Leisure Lifers**: Those whose goal is a life of continual pleasure and enjoyment backed by the financial resources to achieve such a goal.
- **Anxious Idealists**: Those who are driven to leaving a legacy of "giving back" to society through a life of philanthropy, charity, and volunteerism.
- **Stretched and Stressed**: Those who are living from paycheck to paycheck and have little savings and no or very uncertain pension prospects.

Where do you see yourself at this time? How do you avoid this last category into which an increasing number of boomers may soon find themselves?

I would describe myself as an early trailblazer who might well have ended up in this last category, with no time freedom, had I not been guided to that successful pension planner. He asked me how much money I would need to live comfortably for the next 20 years. Like many boomers, I had grossly underestimated the savings I would need to achieve my monthly goals. He told me that, to maintain the standard of living I was accustomed to, I would need almost 20 times my annual income in financial wealth! A boomer earning $50,000 a year at retirement would need about $1 million beyond whatever they earned from Social Security. If they had an income-producing partner and had paid off their house, they would obviously need less. But the magnitude of the challenge still astounded me.

Nor had I thought through the other major challenges we boomers now face as we move into the next phase of our lives, the "renewal age." We actually need to respond to four aspects of our future wellbeing: personal, physical, financial, and environmental.

Personal Wellbeing

First, like other trailblazers, I concluded that I needed to redefine retirement. My career as a business owner, therapist, and spiritual director had allowed me to focus on both the inner and outer aspects of my life. My businesses, however, had cultivated my extroverted self to the detriment of my introverted self. The challenge was to recreate a work focus that would leverage more time for the inner me. As a wealth builder, I continued to find a sense of purpose and direction in my work, but I wanted to find a supplemental, renewable income that would give me time for what really mattered now—being with family, traveling to new places, and accommodating my spiritual and meditative practices.

Finding balance between work and play was essential. Always the caregiver, I also had to understand the balance between self-care and caring for others. It was necessary to go within and redefine my own personal value as I began shifting from valuing myself through my accomplishments to valuing me for who I am.

Recently, I met with parents who were worried that their children seemed happy when people "liked" them and sad when people didn't.

I asked one set of parents to evaluate their response to their daughter who was, at that point, really struggling with this issue. I had them draw a downward-facing triangle and label each corner with the word, "victim," "rescuer," or "villain," essentially conflict resolution/communication 101.

We labeled the downward point "victim," and I asked them where the most power was on this triangle. I remember the wide-eyed look in their eyes as this awareness deepened in them, when I said, "And the difficulty here is that when we respond to the victim this way, we are teaching them *that they do not have* what it takes to make life work." I added, "And we are teaching them that their value can come only from outside of themselves, as from a boyfriend's or girlfriend's approval, for example."

As James Hollis so poignantly states in his book, *Finding Meaning in the Second Half of Life*, "Codependence may or may not be a diagnosis, but it certainly is an estrangement to the soul." I began to imagine how different my life would be if we were taught by society to look inside for our value instead of outside.

Then I heard it myself, as if for the first time and remembered a question we often asked our clients, "Whose life are you living now?" That's when I began consciously to schedule life-giving activities on my calendar so that caring for myself became a priority. I had taught this so many times but, in these last ten years, I had become a professional caregiver for my parents, forgetting about myself in the process. As stewardesses advise, "If traveling with a child, in the case of an emergency, put on your own oxygen mask first." That was the beginning for me of finding balance and wellbeing.

Through the whole spiritual process we learn to dis-illusion ourselves from our false ego. This is a continual process of shedding our illusions the way a snake sheds its skin. We call this process "realization," and the more we identify what really matters to us and live accordingly, the more we activate this process of "realization." The more we allow who we really are to express itself, the more fulfilled and clear we become.

Physical-Social Wellbeing

My second challenge was with issues regarding my physical-social wellbeing. Extended life spans have become both a blessing and a challenge for boomers. Since 1946, the average life span of Americans has increased between 10% according to the U.S. Census Bureau statistics and 12%. In 1946, the first baby boomers had an expected lifespan of 72 to 74 years for men and 75 to78 years for women.

Since then, however, improvements in medicine, nutrition, and personal consciousness have sent average life expectancies into the high 70s for men and into the low- to mid-80s for women. This has affected the tail end of our parent's generation, as well. Indeed, a recent national survey based on U.S. Census Bureau statistics indicates that in Collier County, Florida, where I live, women live to an average age of 86, the longest life expectancy in the country.

Baby boomers are among the healthiest and most health-conscious generation in American history. "Our 70s will be the new 50s," is our widely quoted mantra. Many of us today expect to live well into our 90s, even to reach 100, but not without some significant changes later in life.

This potential longevity may allow us to reframe our dreams, but it also raises three critical questions. First, how do we cope with the "sandwich generation syndrome"? Second, how will we be cared for in our later years? And third, how can we ensure that we don't outlive our money? This last question will be addressed in later chapters.

First, how do we avoid being torn between taking care of aging parents in their 80s and 90s and helping children, between their late 20s and early 40s, who may be challenged financially in the current economy? The pressures of being caregivers (for parents) and/or providers (for children) fall primarily on women. I can personally attest to this. My husband and I took in my parents eight years ago and had to find a larger home. We cared for my father, who had Parkinson's disease and later grappled with Alzheimer's. My mother, who still lives with us, is a sprightly 89 years old, and recently underwent two cornea transplants to restore her sight so that she might be able to continue driving, her last symbol of independence.

It was our legacy as women in my family to take care of others. My mother fully embraced that legacy as she cared for my grandmother, who lived with us for more than 23 years. When my parents downsized, my grandmother then lived with my aunt and she then made her transition at the age of 102. My parents taught me the value of caring for their parents. I never forgot the lesson, and when it seemed time, I stepped up to the plate naturally.

Although I would not trade these years for the memories and lessons they have so richly provided, I have become all too aware that for the first twelve years of our marriage, my husband and I have made personal sacrifices to accommodate this lifestyle of being caregivers. Caregiving affects everyone who says YES to this way of life, including the ones being cared for. I fully advocate receiving support from outside sources to avoid caregiver burnout. I agree with James Hollis, "Family is to support the nurturance and wellbeing of all members, parent and child alike."

This brings up the second question: Who will take care of *me* in my old age?

In fact, this issue is of special concern to female boomers, who are likely to become single through choice, separation, divorce or widowhood. According to reports published in 2012 by the Urban Institute and AARP, of female boomers are single at this time, up from 30% in 1989 . For those who entered the work force after 1960, they typically earned 25% to 30% less than their male counterparts, often went back to work after motherhood, and had less time to invest in pension plans. Many are not prepared financially or psychologically for the long haul of extended life spans.

My stepchildren are wonderful people and well-established professionally, but neither my husband nor I expect them to support us in our final years. I am the youngest person in my household; my husband is eight years older than I am, and my soul sister is six years older. Statistically, I should live longest.

I remember a recent visit to an independent living facility to see my maternal great-aunt who, in her mid-90s, still was dressed impeccably. The lobby was beautiful, but I could not avert my eyes from the gaunt faces of 20 women in their late 80s sitting on couches in silence just waiting...and waiting.... I was overcome with emotion as I imagined what they might be feeling day after day, simply sitting, all dressed up, with seemingly nowhere to go.

The word sacrifice has its root in "sacred." I pray that our devotion to parental care giving has helped us make of the timber of out lives a home that will bless us and turn out waiting into reflections of peace and joy.

Nonetheless, as I look to my elder years, questions about my caregivers and their perspective now take on new meaning. Who will they be? Will they be proactive on my part? Will they respect my wishes? Conscious retirement asks us to answer these questions, to create a Plan B of our making.

Likewise, I am blessed to come from a lineage of parents who were healthy most of their lives. Yet I am continually upgrading my standard of healthy living by taking nutritional supplements that are documented as the most effective in the marketplace, by upgrading my diet to eliminate most sugars and other empty carbohydrates, and to drink quality water, exercise regularly, and sleep well. I also spend a portion of every day in prayer and reflection, quietly replenishing my energy.

Herein lies the challenge... If I believe that by being proactive I can change the quality of my life, this road is worth the challenge. But if I believe "dis-ease" is inevitable, then it probably is.

I believe in being proactive, holistically treating the whole person as well as the parts—body, mind, and spirit. Years ago, in the movie *Oh God*, starring George Burns, he made a poignant statement that can be applied here, "You have everything it takes to make it work."

With regard to the prevention of disease, people fall somewhere on a continuum between the medical model, which endorses the treatment of disease, to the holistic model, which endorses the prevention of disease. Our counseling centers were decidedly holistic in their orientation, as we came from the perspective that people have within them the resources "to make their lives work." This "integrative" perspective on contemporary caring and healing is crucial to our case in our elder years.

Financial Wellbeing

One of the greatest concerns among many boomers is long-term health care and how to pay for it. How do we prevent or detect the early onset of a major disease or illness, and ensure that our money lasts at least as long as we do?

Financial wellbeing for most boomers is the foundation of their retirement dreams. Yet several studies have shown that *only 1 in 3 boomers are prepared for their financial future.* In no other category of wellbeing has our song changed so dramatically. When I was younger, I was taught not only that hard work and a college education and beyond would ensure the good life, but that buying a home, a car (or perhaps two), and having savings in the bank were testimony to the Great American Dream. We are now in the midst of a financial environment, challenging the American Dream, in which homes and savings are not worth what they used to be, while health care and energy costs seem to continue to rise steadily.

Many 401(k)s are now 201(k)s, worth far less than before the stock market crash of 2007. Employers saw 401(k) plans as cheaper to maintain than traditional pensions, but many employees were naïve and uninformed investors who paid little attention to their investment reports, assuming a profitable return when they needed supplementary retirement funds after age 65. As a report on CBS's *60 Minutes* announced in December 2011, more than 30 million prospective retirees have lost between 30% and 50% of their 401(k) funds during the past ten years. They now face federal taxes on their dwindling 401(k)s after they reach 70 years, six months during the next decade. And they will face creeping inflation, which has averaged 2.5% annually during the past decade (which means that $100 today will be worth only $61 in twenty years' time).

Several investment reports from the Federal Reserve Bank, Merrill Lynch, and MetLife, now indicate that more than half of all early boomers in the lowest income bracket, below $12,000 a year, will run out of money before they reach 75. The average Social Security check pays out only $1,170 a month or $14,000 annually. *It's astounding that 20% of married retirees and 40% of single retirees currently depend on Social Security for 90% of their income.* What matters most to them is daily survival rather than long-term comfort.

Many later boomers (reaching 66-plus after 2021) are aware that the Social Security and Medicare systems may be much less viable and secure when they plan to retire. Such a tenuous future means that an increasing proportion of retirees cannot retire, but will be forced to continue to work or to be rehired in a less favorable working environment for older employees. You can observe this phenomenon already at your local supermarket and other big-box stores, smaller retail stores, restaurants, and hotels. And you will see it clearly in our future lifestyles as we channel our available cash flows.

Environmental Wellbeing

Such financial challenges deeply affect our environmental wellbeing, especially our residential choices. What will constitute my "home" in my later years? Most of us want to live "at home" as long as possible and make our own choices about being cared for as we age. For early boomers, this might seem a most unlikely outcome down the road, but being prepared is crucial and having a Plan B has never been more essential. Those of us with children or grandchildren wonder, *When we reach our 80s will they want to help us? Will they be financially able to help us?* The last thing we baby boomers want to be is a burden on our families. We are fiercely independent.

The most fortunate are not only the wealthy for whom residential choices are widely available, but also those, married or single, who are fortunate to have lived long enough to pay off their mortgages. A home mortgage generally has constituted 35 to 40% of basic monthly expenses. Years ago, a couple had a built-in savings plan if their mortgage was paid off. Yet, because of divorce, remarriage, and delayed home purchase, only 20 to 25% of early boomers aged 65 to 74 have their homes paid off and only another 10% will have theirs eliminated by the time they are 75.

For those renting and unlikely to own a home again, there is the probability of steadily increasing rents for the rest of their lives—a sobering prospect. In a deeply depressed housing market, however, many boomer "nest eggs" have disappeared for the foreseeable future and a growing numbers of retirees face the prospect of foreclosure. Between 2007 and 2011, based on a study by AARP, 1.5 million Americans over the age of 50 lost their homes to foreclosure. Millions of older Americans are carrying considerable mortgage debt. And more than 3 million are at risk of losing their homes in the immediate future because their prime loans are due.

The greater one's wealth, and the better one's health, the greater the residential choices available to us. *Wealth plus health equals choices.*

The wealth builders and the leisure lifers may not be as focused upon residential wellbeing as other boomer categories. But the age cohort born 10 to 15 years before the early boomers has already blazed trails here. Continuing Care Retirement Communities (CCRCs) have sprung up across the country. With "buy-ins" varying from $150,000 to $500,000 per person, such communities provide residential arrangements for progressive aging from independent living (villas, condominiums, apartments) to assisted-living units and full-time nursing care, all in the same residential environment. They provide a sense of wellbeing and security, especially for female survivors who tend to be more socialized, more independent, and more able to cope with advancing age than men. Such communal arrangements with like-minded boomers, whether owning or renting, are likely to become more popular during the next 20 years, provided that people have streams of income to support that lifestyle.

Alternatively, "continuing care at home" arrangements are likely to appeal to independently minded boomers. According to a recent Associated Press-Life Goes Strong.com survey, 52% of baby boomers indicated that they were unlikely to move to a new living space after retirement. Public funding for such "aging in place" choices is often available, especially in specific housing developments or larger neighborhoods that can attract specialized support services such as transportation and home health care. Seniors still living at home, however, can buy memberships to continuing-care communities and have access to dining and health-care services while staying in their own homes. In some states, home-based seniors can reserve the right to move into a CCRC at a later date with funds previously placed in escrow for that specific purpose.

It is also important to know what support services are available in your own locality, your county or municipality. What information is readily available on community centers, health services, adult educational opportunities, transportation, fire and ambulance services, music, the arts, and entertainment, and the like? In Collier County, Florida, where I live, older residents who don't own a car or can no longer drive, or who find public transportation unavailable or inconvenient, can use a locally subsidized Para Transit system to get around for a nominal fee. Such a system does not exist in all Florida counties. Similarly, the quality of services varies significantly from place to place, which may directly impact your wellbeing. Be fully informed about your local services.

In view of the equation "wealth plus health equals choices," it is crucial for all boomers to plan ahead for retirement security. Our wellbeing is our "senior freedom." Making time for what matters, creating a residual income, and living a legacy are the clearest expressions of that freedom.

"Joy does not simply
happen to us. We
have to choose joy
and keep choosing it
every day."

Henri J.W. Nouwen

Chapter 3

Developing Insight: Conscious Retirement

It was 8:15 p.m. when I was called to the home of one of my oncology patients to be with her. We had met previously in the hospital and had hoped for a different outcome after her months of treatment. I knew this was a distress call and I wanted to keep my promise to be there for her.

When my husband and I arrived, she knew the time had come to say goodbye. I held her hand gently and tenderly. She asked me to go upstairs and be with her 3-year-old son and her husband, neither of whom I had met before.

She said, "I painted my son's room so he'll grow up with remembering my love." How she had ever found the energy to paint the messages on his wall, I will never know, but as I switched on the light to his room, I stood there in awe. There, amidst the Sesame Street characters, were words of love from a mother to her child, "Remember you matter." "You are a precious and wonderful person." "I will always love you." I will never forget that experience nor the message she left us all: Remember to make time for what matters...now.

I make time, especially when I speak to women, to see if they are living their dream now. Most of them wish they could maintain the money, the time, and the good health to enjoy their prosperity. Busy-ness, however, seems to be the mode of operation for so many people today and it leaves me wondering, "What will it take to turn this seeming madness around?"

Let me provide another perspective on this issue. Mary was the mother of twins, both of whom were 7 years old. We met one-on-one many times, and with the girls and her family, a few times. Always willing to live on the edge, Mary used the challenge of her cancer as an impetus to enjoy every moment with her family. She enjoyed remission for a year, sought treatment and then again enjoyed remission for many months. She was clear with her children about the challenge before them as a family and prepared the way for their aunt and grandfather to care for them. While visiting Mary during her final week, she asked me to pray for her by placing my hand on her heart. "My only regret," she said, "is that I wished I had more time to see the children grow up. I know that they know that they are loved. We have made the most of this time together."

In the past, I saw my success as a straight line upward, as if on a graph, on my way from goal accomplishment to goal accomplishment. Now, I see my life as a circle with spokes generating out from the center. This indicates that my relationship to my Higher Power, myself, my family and friends, and my business partners, guides my decisions about my work schedule. My work is important to me, but only in that it serves my personal wellbeing and enriches the evolution of my relationships.

Creating a Plan B

When you visualize your future and consider a Plan B, is it enough to generate additional income, even if it meant you would have to sacrifice the quality of your relationships to keep that money coming in? For me, that answer was, obviously, no way!

As a wedding planner and officiant, establishing a Plan B is crucial. Such a plan is defined as a place for shelter from inclement weather on a beach or other open space. Every couple who works with us is encouraged to have a Plan B.

My personal Plan B would have to help me create time as well as money, while enhancing my life. Likewise, my Plan B had to serve others as well as myself. So if you are passionate about helping others, you will appreciate what you are about to read.

In an earlier chapter I referred to a perspective a young girl held regarding her hopes for affection, and how, if she failed to turn that around to something more positive, she may resign herself to a life of worthlessness. A parallel exists for boomers who want to *live well and prosper* in their renewal years by honoring their dreams. Lynn Hall wrote, "*We do not change as we grow older, we simply become* more clearly ourselves."

How will you welcome the gift of seeing yourself clearly, so that your future unfurls *your* dream, not someone else's dream, but yours?

I define "conscious retirement" as the creation of a new purposeful way of life, one over which *we* can exert control. It is being open to seeing more clearly who we are and to take action that will be "full-filling."

Many boomers who want to increase their retirement funding are only seeking work that provides meaning in their lives. I recently spoke to a boomer who is still working, but asking the question: "At the end of the day, how did my work enhance anyone's life?" Conscious retirement asks us to reflect upon that question.

A 2012 MetLife-Civic Ventures study revealed that 31 million people aged 44 to 70 years want an additional career, or "encore career," one that has personal meaning, continued income, and creates some social impact. "Some 53% of those interviewed went back to work because of insufficient income or dwindling savings." At the same time, 47% sought additional education or job retraining, or enrolled in volunteer programs that might provide experiences allowing entry into new work experiences.

A dear friend of mine, a boomer who lives alone in an opulent country home, asks, "How do I bridge the gap between loneliness and being alone in my renewal years?" Conscious retirement means we come to grips with that question.

Many people in relationships can attest to the fact that you can be equally lonely in a relationship or actually being alone. Many professionals are super-successful in the eyes of their peers and colleagues, but on the inside may experience great isolation and/or loneliness. And no boomer wants their renewal years to be marked by loneliness.

- My Plan B: Ensured a team approach to working, so I could draw upon my strengths and the strengths of others, bridging the gap to that seeming isolation of working in a vacuum.
- Encouraged me to find a business model that would allow for

the flexibility to care for my family and my aging parents at home. So working from home with flexible hours was essential.

- Had to be centered on providing me with income even when I did NOT work. Making time for what matters was more than the name of my business, it was my passion and I wanted to experience my passion.

My training as a therapist and spiritual director guided me again to James Hollis' book, *Finding Meaning in the Second Half of Life*. He quotes a favorite poet of mine, Rainer Maria Rilke: "and then the knowledge comes to me that I have 'space' within me for a second, 'timeless,' larger life." My larger vision would unfurl only as I made time to live it.

Earlier this summer, I read two obituaries in the *New York Times* about women I did not know. What was written spoke to me deeply. One stated: "She had a natural ability to interact with children, having never lost her sense of wonder." The other read: "She was an artist in understanding and transforming others."

These tender tributes touched a chord within me. I never gave much thought to obituaries, much less writing or reading them, until three years ago when my dad died and my husband penned his obituary. I heard people's responses to what he wrote and saw how those words brought my dad's spirit to life.

In all the years of doing therapy, taking supervision, and teaching workshops on healing, I remember an invitation to write my own obituary. I thought it premature then, but now I know better. Now I appreciate the intention behind that suggestion.

Perhaps if we begin with what, to many people, seems like "the end in mind," we could evaluate our lives, regroup, and move forward in a new way. One of my practices in the morning, before speaking with anyone, is to meditate upon who I am today and how I am living my life in accordance with my values. Reflecting on my life daily helps me put things in perspective and claim my good every day.

As a spiritual practice, turning our loneliness into solitude can benefit our boomer years. As an introvert, I am at home with silence, and that silence can lead me to solitude. Solitude that makes time for what really matters often leaves one feeling full, not lonely. Silence and solitude can be hard to come by unless one makes a deliberate attempt to preserve them in one's busy life. Making time for contemplation and reflection really matters.

During that time, meditating or reading inspirational books, like those written by Henri Nouwen or Eric Butterworth, is fulfilling. Sometimes I listen to a prerecorded meditation, especially those created by Unity Church. Whatever the medium, time in solitude offers a renewed peace of mind to face the day. Other boomers may achieve this centeredness through walking, jogging, or going to the gym. But whatever the practice, it provides us with a focus for the rest of the day.

In the book, *Ask and You Shall Receive*, authors, Esther and Jerry Hicks, defined "setpoint" as a "perceived limit on our happiness, our time, our money, our love/life." I tease people, saying that as a "forceps" baby, I began this chapter of my life on someone else's time. Although I was born two weeks late, I always felt like my time was someone else's call. Applying the Hicks' metaphor, I might have a "setpoint" regarding time operating in my life. Our beliefs and the 100,000 hours (at least 12 years) of conditioning in childhood help to "seemingly" cement these setpoints in place.

Our language can often be a clue as to the beliefs we hold, beliefs that have a definite effect on our setpoints. As an example, my husband remembers as a child watching his mother cleaning the house, look at him and remark, "How is the enemy?" This was her way of asking what time it was. That attitude caused my husband to explore his setpoint and beliefs about time. Much to my advantage, he did. To this day, I can count on him to keep me focused on "the now" as the most precious moment; in this way I approach time as my friend, not my enemy.

My values meditation asks these four questions :

- What do you value?
- What are your motivations?
- What is your heart's desire?
- How would you like to be?

Conscious retirement requests that we allow questions like these to guide us up and away from those thoughts and beliefs that could otherwise keep us "stuck" in our setpoints. If you are not where you want to be in your relationship with time or money or love or happiness, I urge you to make the time to allow these questions to help you discover new dimensions of yourself at this point in your journey.

One of my spiritual directors once asked, "How would it be if we continue to prioritize other aspects of our lives to the exclusion of nurturing our spiritual wellbeing?" I see spiritual wellbeing as the type of discernment whereby we become conscious of our thoughts, beliefs, and actions in our daily lives. Over and over again, the many circumstances in my life have been calling me to observe myself and transition to a new way of thinking rather than spend time resolving a situation, which may have no worthwhile outcome.

Because work is a comfortable place for me and always has been, it's as if I have used the path of commerce as a great step in personal evolution. Being in the helping professions in one way or another for my first and second careers has been a blessing. Through my counseling centers, my professional speaking, and my spiritual direction, I have been allowed to enter into my clients' inner worlds where so many others would not be privileged to go.

Through my work in business development, I have been privileged to accompany other entrepreneurs who prioritize wellness: personal, financial, environmental, and spiritual. On this journey, I have found untold reward as a mentor and leader in the process of helping others live well and prosper. What follows is a glimpse of my own process toward conscious retirement.

In 2005, I accepted a two-year position of leadership with a women's organization in town. As president of that networking organization, I worked an average of 20 hours per week. The group was in growth mode and so was I. My husband questioned why I would agree to guide its growth at a time when two new companies I had founded were also in growth mode, demanding so much of my time and energy. I knew he was helping me identify my "why," and clarify my purpose and I was open to uncovering the answer to both.

When my term as president was over, I reflected on the experience with the hope of knowing what the true gifts of that service were for me. I refocused my energy exclusively on building my wellness company and achieved a high status of senior director, my long-term financial goal at the time. Likewise, that same year we were blessed that our wedding-planning company was selected as a preferred vendor with several of the most prestigious five-star resorts in town. Blessing was everywhere.

I asked myself many times: What if I had focused my energy solely on building my companies instead of accepting the position as president of a women's organization? Was that decision a reaction to a setpoint I held for success or was it a response to something deeper within me?

The answer became clearer with time. My not-for-profit service as president provided me with the time and "space" to create that inner vision of me that would be the force behind my subsequent fulfillment in life. Likewise, that renewed vision gave me strength of character for still another chapter in my life, which would ask me to dig deeper into those resources of strength than I ever knew existed.

I supported my father as he continued his journey and transition through a challenge of seven years with Parkinson's, dementia, and eventually Alzheimer's disease (in the form of Lewy Body Disease), and that newfound vision would be my guide. I will share more about this experience later in the final chapter as I speak about living your legacy. For now, let me say that our challenges are often blessings in disguise and we must embrace them with the wisdom that comes from being open to new opportunities to expand our lives.

"Out beyond ideas
of wrong-doing and
right-doing there is a
field. I'll meet
you there."

Rumi

Chapter 4

Living a Legacy

As I wrote in chapter 2, retirement for boomers will last longer than retirement did for their parents. According to the U.S. Census Bureau, the number of people aged 65 and older in the United States (not just boomers) will at least double by 2050. This will bring the numbers from 39 million to 89 million or approximately 30% of our total population. A rather startling fact is that some of us will have more years in retirement than we spent in the workforce!

The idea of living longer is matched for boomers only by the idea of living *healthier* and longer lives. Many boomers have witnessed, as I have, the long suffering of the diseases of their parents, family and friends, and pray that living longer, healthier lives is our inheritance.

A longer, healthier life must be supported by a healthier portfolio and wealthier financial position. The question one asks is identical to one my esthetician asked me recently, "How do boomers create the kind of income it takes to ensure that they will not outlive their money?" I had asked the same question of my financial planner, so I knew the challenge before me. To ensure that my income beyond Social Security would represent having at least $1 million in savings, I needed to receive $5,000 in dividends or their equivalent every month.

To that end, my husband and I made a major and bold decision to move permanently to Florida. We sold our Victorian home in Rhode Island and built a new home in Naples. Our new vision mandated a new beginning but, from a business perspective, it proved to be a major challenge. First, we had established our wellness business in Rhode Island for 15 years and leaving New England meant a loosening of connections with our regional clientele and referral sources. This new business plan would offer the establishment of a residual income that we envisioned in our 15-year plan. With a residual income, we would be compensated regularly for a service we provided only once. Moving to Florida meant finding an additional set of new contacts. I had always been a good networker and I jumped into the established network organizations in Southwest Florida, while creating strong relationships.

These early contacts not only built up our wellness business, but also created an opportunity for a second stream of income. My therapeutic and spiritual direction expertise allowed us to enter the thriving wedding-planning business specializing in destination, beach, and country club weddings. Our business, A Beautiful Florida Wedding, was born. No matter the state of the economy, people still fall in love and want to get married, renew their vows, baptize their children. This income stream was transactional, like the counseling centers, where we were paid once for the services we provided.

We had entered our second or "encore" careers. But to keep things in perspective, allow me to tell you about the success of our wellness company. It was August 2009, and I was vacationing with my husband. I had just become a senior director with the wellness company and awaited my bonus check as a reward for my achievement. Our regular check had been paying for our monthly mortgage and seven other line items. This additional check would be deposited in our savings account. Imagine my joy and my astonishment when it arrived and my colleague, Catherine, exclaimed, "Do you realize that this check is equal to what we would be paid to officiate 30 weddings?!" I was extremely fortunate to have a propensity towards planning the future and I was doubly blessed to be surrounded by experts who inspired me to create that Plan B when I did.

I have come to realize, however, that retirement for many boomers is far from this dream come true. As we are all too aware, financial setbacks have forced increasing numbers of boomers to rethink retirement and to continue to work indefinitely so that they don't become further stretched and stressed. They have become the working wounded, the rehired, or the retrained.

The trends are startling. The proportion of workers 65 and older in the labor force increased from 10.8% in 1985 to 17.4% in 2010. Between 2007 and 2010, the number of older workers increased by 16%. In 2011, 36.5% of 65- to 69-year-old men and almost 35% of women in the same age bracket are working, increasingly as full-time, rather than part-time workers. Currently, 450,000 Americans 65 and older are looking for work. This number has doubled since 2007, according to the 2012 MetLife-Civic Ventures report.

At the same time, we boomers have hardly been paragons of thrift. We have saved less than 4% of our incomes every year since the beginning of the century. And this in light of the fact that the net worth of 55- to 64-year-olds has decreased from $273,000 (including housing) in 2008 to less than $230,000 today. The times cry out for new lines of enterprise and new means of self-employment, where entrepreneurs have control over their work hours and conditions.

As Edward Glaeser, an economics professor at Harvard University, wrote recently, "Gradually, our image of 70-year-olds needs to change from Florida retirees to Florida entrepreneurs, who find ways to make a bit of cash doing something a bit more fun than their former work." Finding a fulfilling life in a new work ethic and a new mode of activity may be the solution that boomers seek.

So how does one proceed?

A Reliable Residual Income

My experiences have given me some insights into what kind of self-employment can be a fulfilling option. Many people find it difficult to begin a business from scratch with little capital investment. One option is to associate with a company, as I did, that has an impeccable reputation and whose compensation program rewards cooperation rather than creating stress through competition.

In our workshops, we help boomers identify the qualities of companies that can enhance their lives. We also help them identify aspects of work-from-home businesses to avoid.

I am a testimony to the fact that companies do exist that provide a fulfilling and financially rewarding experience. These are not unsustainable get-rich-quick schemes, but solid business enterprises based on a business model that leverages the time and expertise of a team. Members draw on each other's strengths and encouragements; all participants benefit financially, emotionally, and spiritually.

The financial landscape for older Americans, as we have seen, continues to be a very troublesome one. According to 2012 estimates , made by AARP, MetLife, and the New York Times:

- 75% of Americans reaching retirement age have less than $30,000 in retirement accounts.
- 50% of households headed by people ages 65 to 74 have no money in retirement accounts.
- Almost 5% of middle-class workers will be poor or near poor in retirement.
- Working longer is unlikely to be very remunerative.
  - Unemployment rates for those aged 50 and older are the higher than any other age group. Displaced older workers find themselves in minimum-wage jobs, without health coverage or are chronically unemployed.
- Retirement based on voluntary savings is unrealistic—at age 55, a prospective retiree needs to save 30% of annual earnings to have a secure retirement. How many of us have that kind of fortitude?

In sum, it appears that downward socio-economic mobility and chronic indebtedness loom on the horizon unless we can generate a more sustainable income. Even as intelligent, well-educated boomers, we are not immune to the challenge of the current financial crisis.

Thinking through a "Plan B" twelve years ago has saved us during this time of volatile global economy. We were not "upside down" in our real estate, and we did not have risky investments, yet here we are still asking the question: Where do we go from here? Because we decided to replace our transactional income counseling company with a "residual income" wellness company, we are able to enjoy financial stability and peace of mind. *How are we ever going to get more time in our lives unless we stop trading time for dollars with jobs that pay us only when we work?*

If I could stand on a rooftop and shout a message for all to hear, I would exclaim "living a legacy requires time and the money to enjoy it." I believe our future as boomers who want to create additional income in the 21st century rests with businesses that must generate residual income. I am not referring to businesses that require a sharp learning curve like insurance or financial planning, which would be great options at a younger age, nor am I speaking of participation in multilevel-marketing models that promise much at considerable personal and financial risk.

Unlocking the Prosperity Code

Understanding four principles will help you form your own plan. They are Money, Prevention, Spirituality and Environment.

Principles of Money

- Transactional income will always keep you working. (You only get paid when you work.)
- Jobs will never give you time freedom.
- It's not how much you make, it's how much you keep.
- You must find a way to multiply and duplicate your efforts, in order to compound your income.
- "Home Operated Businesses" also maximize your ability to obtain all the tax benefits you are entitled to receive.

Principles of Prevention

- The old adage, "An ounce of prevention is worth a pound of cure" is true.
- It's much easier to stay well than to get well if we become ill.
- Our medical system can't be the caretaker of our body and our earth. We must be proactive in our own health care.
- Our immune system responds to our level of stress.

Principles of Spirituality: Living a Legacy

- What we hold in mind, duplicates in kind.
- Staying in the flow of life requires that we release our negative thoughts (such as poverty and illness) and affirm positive ones (prosperity and health).
- Spiritual processes are at work in our lives; believe that you can career experience in which the "need to work" stage is becoming

- overcome seemingly impossible challenges.
- Knowing who you are and your vision for life, are the keys to prosperity.

Principles of Environment:
- Wealth plus health equals environmental choices
- Our wellbeing is our senior freedom – live healthy and prosper
- Caregiving affects everyone who participates in this lifestyle
- Plan ahead for your own final residential choice

As a professional speaker and as a wedding planner, transactional income comes from my speaking engagements and my services. Residual income, with time freedom, has come only from my aligning myself with a national company whose brand and mission I am passionate about. In this manner, I can broker the company in the marketplace by making referrals regularly and being paid for them on a continual basis. For me, *"time freedom" is the new collateral of retirement well lived.*

In Ken Dychtwald's book *Age Power,* he states, "As boomers move toward the second half of their lives, they shift their perspective from lives of success to lives of significance." For boomers in transition, our purpose is to transform lives, including our own. *The invitation of our renewal years is that we must become deliberate in our choices to do so.*

My 12-year plan to semi-retirement has come to fruition. Just recently, I gifted myself with the luxury of being with my family for the entire summer, most of it on vacation. And for four weeks I enjoyed time with them on the beach, simply reveling in the exquisite gifts of nature. I have already established a not-for-profit foundation, the Lamplighter Legacy Fund, which contributes to the lives of caregivers, especially daughters of Alzheimer's patients, and is partially funded by my residual income. A residual income gives me the financial security, peace of mind, and freedom to do what I want when I want. When I, too, may want a caregiver to support me, I will be able to utilize the funds generated by my several streams of income.

Many boomers are in the process of caring for their personal wellbeing and rethinking their future. This process is creating a new the "passion to live" mode. My next goal is to prepare the way to honor the thought that, no matter our age, we can live our dreams with passion.

In his book *Spiritual Economics*, Eric Butterworth shares that in a study of centenarians, not one was a retired-to-do-nothing person, or in other words, a leisure lifer. He states, "The life change of retirement may be good for you, but only if it is seen not as an end but as a redirection of activities and interests. Truth is we do not grow old, when we stop growing we are old."

When I reflect upon how I am living my legacy, I observe myself approaching each moment with an openness and curiosity, a shift away from being judgmental toward myself to being more loving and forgiving of myself. And although my goals are still important to me in all facets of my life, I am more understanding that they are simply the opportunity for me to express who I really am.

I use the phrase "living a legacy" to describe this way of staying renewed in body, mind and spirit. In the past, we have heard about "leaving" a legacy, whether in the form of an estate, a reputation, a living will or trust. But I believe, given our character as a group, we boomers are equally interested in "living a legacy." Living your legacy now is an invitation to differentiate yourself from what appears to be your circumstances in life, to define the real meaning and opportunity for transformation that those circumstances offer.

According to a recent report published by the National Alzheimer's Association, "Too many boomers may spend their retirement years either with Alzheimer's or caring for someone who has it." It is likely that, unless we find a cure for the disease, Alzheimer's may become the defining disease of the Baby Boomer generation. According to the association's most recent report, at least one in eight boomers could be challenged in this way by age 65. At age 85, that rate could increase dramatically to nearly one in two.

A clear example of Living a Legacy was demonstrated by my dad as he made his transition through Parkinson's disease, early dementia, and Alzheimer's disease. My father's odyssey began with the typical shuffling and falling that heralds the onset of Parkinson's. Then came the onset of depression, memory loss, and dramatic changes in behavior.

Eventually my father had to stop driving, then he stopped walking, then he stopped getting out of bed. Yet even when he was virtually immobile and silent, he continued to live his legacy. This was most apparent when music therapy was added to his treatment. Suddenly, out of the silence, came his rendition of Al Jolson (whom my father had played in vaudeville) singing "Glory to God in the Highest." I will never forget that moment, nor his legacy that continued well after his chronological age of 88.

I look back on the everyday with my father, my mentor, and feel tremendous gratitude for his presence in my life! Everyone knew him as a character whose humor and goodness had touched their lives. These days, as I approach my renewal years, I think of him and his joy. My dad lived his legacy of joy, which continues to influence my life today. I honor it through my Lamplighter Legacy Fund (my father had been in the lighting business), which is my way of giving back to my community.

I remember one of my teachers sharing three tenets that challenged my thinking about life:

- Circumstances are not what they appear to be.
- God, or Spirit, or the Universe is so much larger than we think.
- I AM so much more than my outer self.

Let's develop each of those on our way to indentifying how You can LIVE Your legacy.

Circumstances are not what they seem.

Years ago, I experienced that serving a not-for-profit networking organization for women's businesses proved to reveal so much more. Unity Church presents a concept that I call "waiting for manifestation." This can be described as what happens between the times we seek results, while believing in the power of affirmative prayer. When we say that circumstances are not what they seem, we move from a position of powerlessness to a position of waiting with the belief that everything has a season.

God is so much more than we think.

As a child I was taught about a God "up there" and prayed constantly "to" that God, regularly attending services where people believed as I did. As an adult, I was blessed with spiritual mentors who believed in the presence of God within.

Later in life, I discovered how God expresses through me: beauty, truth, integrity, courage, and love and have always appreciated the 12-step phrase "God of my understanding." Thanks to my experience in Unity, I now know I am in control of my outcomes in life.

We are so much more than our outer selves.

In order to LIVE our LEGACY we must uncover our illusions of who we are and prioritize what really matters. When we dis-illusion these three illusions from our thinking, we are open to identify our legacy.

All my life, I have been predisposed to experiencing fulfillment from caregiving. Living my legacy asks me to apply that Spirit to myself in such a way as to inspire others to do the same.

A story here may help make an invitation to "living a legacy" more concrete. It was October 2008 and the hospice social worker had come to visit my dad. One year earlier, I had made plans for a trip to see my husband's family, but now thought about canceling the trip. The social worker felt my anguish and offered some wisdom. "Have you ever read the book *The Four Things That Matter Most* by Ira Byok, a hospice chaplain?" she asked.

"No," I said, "but why do you ask?"

"I know you are feeling torn about leaving your dad, so I'll bring a copy tomorrow."

After reading the book, I felt freer inside to let my dad move on, and I was more at peace to go to Scotland. The book instructs us to complete our goodbyes by addressing our loved one in transition with four sentiments. The first sentiment is to ask forgiveness; the second, to offer forgiveness; the third, to appreciate the way that person's life touched yours; and the fourth, to give permission for our loved ones to move on.

What do these sentiments help us put in place as we boomers prepare for the day when we will reflect on these questions?

Living our legacy comes with the awareness that has been a hallmark of the boomer generation: "now matters." On moving day, we left our dream home to head to our new small condo. Although I knew we were "rightsizing" and solidifying our commitment to apply our resources to what matters to us, I heard myself saying out loud, "Well, we are now beginning the home stretch." I remember my spiritual director once reminding me, a NO to something or someone, especially to yourself, though seemingly bittersweet, can ultimately be a resounding YES to life. This is what I mean when I encourage you to live your legacy now.

What do these sentiments help us put in place as we boomers prepare for the day when we will reflect on these questions?

In his book, *In the Flow of Life*, Eric Butterworth wrote, "All that is required is that we keep in the flow, keep open in mind and heart, by positive thoughts and creative faith, and that we keep moving in the direction of our dreams."

As the book of Matthew says, "For where your treasure is there your heart will be also" (6:21). If you value time alone, you'll find your treasure making time for that. If you value time with family or friends, you'll find your treasure making time for that. Conscious retirement opens the door to living that treasured life.

I hope that this book has opened you to the path of wellbeing in your own life. If you came to this book with the question, "Where do I go from here?" I hope I helped you to take your next step. My husband and I, and people just like you all around the world, are Living a Legacy and Loving it. Now it's your turn. If you are ready to take action and develop a strategy like mine I invite you to take the next step with us by becoming a part of our growing community www.LivingaLegacyandLovingit.com. You also can reach us on Facebook at Facebook.com/livingalegacyandlovingit. The decision you make about where you go from here is entirely your own, and it will be my privilege to assist you along the way.

Cynthia Mitchell is the oldest of three children, and only daughter, born in 1949 into the second-generation Italian-American family of Rita and Hank Imondi. Her mother was a hard-working wife among the first in her generation to also work outside the home. Her father, third of 11 children, was a flight engineer who flew 33 missions in the South Pacific during World War II. A consummate entrepreneur and salesperson, he owned a retail lighting business, many years after managing one for a large corporation.

Cynthia was fortunate to be the first in her family to attend college. She broke the cycle of Italian-American women graduating high school, finding a job, getting married, having children, and serving the family.

Cynthia attended Classical High School in Providence, R.I., and then made a conscious decision to stay close to home and attend the University of Rhode Island. She graduated with a double degree in math and French, and received her Master's degree in counseling from Providence College.

She moved quickly from teaching to guidance counseling, before establishing her own counseling centers, one in Rhode Island and one on Long Island, which she maintained for more than 20 years. At the same time, her heart guided her to pursue a five-year training program and internship as a spiritual director at Our Lady of Peace Spiritual Life Center in Narragansett, R.I. With this training and experience, Cynthia also opened the Institute for Healing and Wholeness, whose curriculum honored both traditional and holistic healing principles. The institute catapulted her into a professional speaking career, which led her eventually to the Program in Women's Oncology affiliated with Rhode Island Hospital. This association changed the course of her career.

After working in a program with women's oncology, Cynthia felt compelled to draw her line in the sand and create a new direction in life, one that would ensure financial wellbeing in retirement while providing her with time to savor life's precious moments. To this day, that decision is making all the difference in the quality of her life and, ultimately, for her retirement.

Cynthia has been recognized for her business, counseling, and leadership skills by such national women's organizations as the National Association of Female Executives and Entrepreneurs (NAFE), regional organizations such as the Small Business Development Center of Southwest Florida, and locally by such women's organizations as the Women's Network of Collier County (WNOCC), where she served two terms as director and president. In her activist role, she also served as a local vice president of Equal Voice for Women as part of her NAFE association.

Currently, Cynthia is founder and president of two businesses: Time for What Matters and A Beautiful Florida Wedding. She started both businesses in Florida as second-career choices in 2000, while in her early 50s. They have allowed her to expand her energy and expertise in the worlds of both wellness and wedding planning.

It is these life experiences and her reflections on achieving a prosperous retirement that inspired her to write this book.

Cynthia Mitchell is also known as "The Time Gifter." As the name of her business implies, she is passionate about helping people who want to create "time for what matters." Her career as entrepreneur, professional speaker, counselor, and spiritual mentor has inspired her to consistently "right-size" her life so that it continually reflects her values. She is particularly excited about working with boomers and others who are preparing for or entering their "renewal years." Her message exhorts us to "Live our legacy now."

After years of working with people searching for meaning in their lives, Cynthia adopted what is now known as "the prosperity code." Her equation "health plus wealth equals choices," is a no-nonsense approach to taking responsibility for our lives.